Cosplay Girls

JAPAN'S LIVE ANIMATION HEROINES

Cosplay Girls

Text and illustrations © 2003 by cocoro books.

All Rights Reserved. No part of this publication may be reproduced,
stored in a retrieval system, or transmitted in any form or by any means, electronic,
mechanical, photocopying, recording, or otherwise without the written consent of the publisher.

Published by DH Publishing Inc.
Address: 2-3-3F Kanda Jimbocho, Chiyoda-ku, Tokyo 101-0051 Japan
www.dhp-online.com

cocoro books is an imprint of DH Publishing Inc.

ISBN 0-9723124-2-0
LIBRARY OF CONGRESS CATALOG NUMBER 2002116056
Printed in China.

Printed by C&C Offset Printing Co., Ltd.
Producers: Koichi Okamoto, Hiroshi Yokoi
Director: Clive Victor France
Designer: Ichie Takahashi
Senior Editors: Takako Aoyama, Jennifer Cahill
Editors: Tomoko Sakashita, Tomokazu Nagai, Yuki Wada, Shinichiro Nakano
Photographers: Hidetoshi Shimazaki, Makoto Mizota
Models: Yuzuru, Jan Kurotaki, Kairi Nagakura, Yaharu Nanjo, KAZUSA
Special thanks to Essai Ushijima

CONTENTS

INTRODUCTION	4
LUM	6
CHUN-LI	10
COSPLAY RUNWAY: Action Heroes	13
COSPLAY RUNWAY: School Spirit	20
COSPLAY RUNWAY: Sweet Things	23
COSPLAY RUNWAY: Sci Fi	31
CUTIE HONEY	34
COSPLAY RUNWAY: Animal Kingdom	39
COSPLAY RUNWAY: Gothic&Lolita	44
MISHA	48
Cosplay Coffee Shop	52
COSPLAY RUNWAY: Asian Style	53
COSPLAY RUNWAY: Pin-Up Girls	60
REI AYANAMI	62
Cosplay Boutique	64
COSPLAY RUNWAY: Stranger Than Fashion	65
Backstage	72
Cosplayers at Home	74
Do-It-Yourself	78
Both Sides of the Camera	82
Cosplay Lingo	84
Essai's Scrapbook: Cosplay Then and Now	85
YATTAMAN NI-GO	92

INTRODUCTION

Kawaii

Depending on the context, the word "kawaii" could mean cute, pretty, cool, nicely designed, sweet, sexy, funny, or a hundred other things.

The word is invoked when talking about food, fashion, people, personalities, everything pleasing from Kitty to Gucci. Kawaii is as hard to pin down and as important as "cool," especially to young Japanese women.

Throughout the wildly different images in this book is the presence of and the quest for kawaii. While many of the costumes have elements of sexuality, cosplay (Japanese-English for "costume play") is not about sexual role-playing or fetishes. What it is about is the subject of some debate. Basically, cosplay is dressing up as a character, usually from animation, manga comics, or video games. It is a social hobby, with events and conventions where cosplayers and photographers meet and mingle. But what exactly would drive an otherwise normal person to spend countless hours and hundreds of dollars to go out in public looking like a cartoon cat in a frilly apron?

Escape Artists

For one thing, it's fun to go out in a costume. And certainly there is an element of escapism at work here. Japan's famously rigid society, with its strict roles and rules stressing community over individuality, is in the midst of major changes. With the bursting of the so-called "economic bubble" of the 1980's and the slowly disappearing lifetime employment system, many feel that cosplay is an escape from uncertain times and a rejection of the status quo. Daily concerns about where the country, the world, and you are going can be temporarily put aside in favor of making, wearing, and doing things kawaii. And there's nothing like a lime green wig and a tiger bikini to make a girl stand out in a crowd of office workers and housewives. Just standing out can be an act of rebellion in a culture that prizes harmony. In the world of cosplay, there are always options and possibilities, and the boundaries that stifle in the real world fall away. One's identity and future are not set in stone - the girl in the Bo-Peep dress can zip into a changing room and emerge as a camouflaged action heroine. Girls become boys and vice versa. Cosplayers even take on cos-names that either represent a favorite character or just something fun, like "Mushroom." But while dressing up may be a move away from the mainstream, it's not a leap into anarchy, for cosplay has an established community with its own rules and aesthetics.

Copy Cats

Japan has long had a copy-cat reputation in the West. Western fashions and labels are scooped up and conspicuously consumed with gusto, from designer handbags to jeans and Hip-hop clothes. One could argue that transforming oneself into a video game or animation character is another act of imitation. Just like purchasing an image by covering oneself in designer logos, maybe these women are buying pre-packaged identities.

In the end, how creative is dressing up like someone else, fictional or otherwise? But whatever influence the West has over them, the games, manga comics, and animation upon which the cosplayers draw are mostly made in, by, and for Japan. Some others are Japanese school or work uniforms, and others are completely original designs that are just kawaii fantasies. Also, the vast majority of these costumes are made from scratch at home with sewing machines, fake fur, spandex, plastic bottles, duct tape, glue guns, and imagination. It does require quite a bit of ingenuity to turn a bank teller into a cyborg. The desire to be someone or something else is a familiar enough urge for all of us. All over the world, there are scores of men and women wishing they were the latest

The Cult of *Kawaii*

By Jennifer Cahill

pop star or movie hero. But in the strange realm of otaku, or fanatics, it's possible to put together a costume and go from wanna-be to star, if only for a little while. It's even possible to get a taste of fame posing for the paparazzi at a convention or other cosplay event.

Alter Egos and Secret Identities

One might look at the woman in the Egyptian pharaoh outfit, or the one with the kung fu mini-buns in her hair, and wonder what she was thinking. Good question. As anyone who's ever gone out in a Halloween get-up knows, there is always a little truth (or at least some wishing) in the fictions we put on. That's the fun of it. The characters here run the gamut from animals to uniformed waitresses, but the most popular are the video game characters. Their appeal is easy to see - at once kawaii in their boots and ribbons, and kicking ass with martial arts moves and magical powers. Who doesn't want to be the spunky street-fighting chick who just won't stay down? This desire is even more striking in a country where gender roles are so well defined and the glass ceiling is barely transparent. Another woman may choose to try on a boy's life in a crooked school necktie, or the bikini and pig-tails of a pin-up girl. It's only temporary - a role to play until she goes back to work or school, or until the next identity captures her imagination. The animated images themselves are seductive with all their fantastic colors and designs, and even mundane work uniforms have their own perky kind of kawaii. Granted, the average female anime character could give Barbie a body-image complex. But the emphasis here is on style and presentation, not matching the outlandish cartoon proportions. Any cosplayer worth her salt is always ready to strike a pose and get into character.

Men, of course, also participate in cosplay and all its attending events, but women make up the greater numbers. Some say this is because of the greater variety of female characters. It is impossible to say exactly why each of these very different women are drawn to cosplay, and the mix of drama and playfulness in these pictures is a reflection of their diverse personalities. You may, after finishing this book, decide they are amusing, bold, geeky, subversive, deluded, or just completely nuts. But whether dressed as their inner-selves or polar opposites, they are going all the way with it, which is in a strange way admirable. After all, if you love something, why not wear it? And if you're going to wear it, why not be it?

LUM

Manga comics and anime are enjoyed by Japanese kids and adults alike. Rabid fans, or otaku, rival Trekkies in their devotion to characters like Princess Lum. She's popular among cosplayers partly for her sexy costume.

Special thanks to BroadBand Cafe NEPPALA   JR Koukashita, Kanda-aioitcho, Chiyoda-ku, Tokyo Tel: 03-5298-2711

CHUN-LI

She may look friendly here, but Chun-Li is known the world over as a fighter. You're bound to see a few of her at most cosplay events, but the interpretations vary from ultra-sweet to downright threatening.

COSPLAY RUNWAY
Action Heroes

Why wait for a knight in shining armor when you can be one? These ladies are suited up to save the day as their favorite fighters, both male and female.

Kyouji, 20 years old

This male character is a hero of the popular series featuring battling space robots.

as Amuro Ray from *Mobile Suit Gundam* [ANIMATION] started in 2001 and has 10 costumes

as a hero from *Genso Suikoden* [GAME] started in 2002 and has 3 costumes

Hami, 21 years old

Houga, 24 years old

as Sango from *Inuyasha* [ANIMATION] started in 2002 and has 6 costumes

as Chokou from *Shin Sangoku-musou 2* [GAME] started in 2001 and has 7 costumes

Minako, 24 years old

Cosplay Girls

Action Heroes

Akiichi, 19 years old

as Yuffie Kisaragi from *Kingdom Hearts* [GAME] started in 1998 and has 10 costumes

Sayaka, 21 years old

One of three school girls defending the earth from evil in a flashy cape.

as Hikaru Shidou from *Magic Knight Rayearth* [ANIMATION] started in 1997 and has 100 costumes

Zuke, 24 years old

This game has 108 characters. So many costumes, so little time.

as Masked Man from *Genso Suikoden 3* [GAME] started in 1998 and has many costumes

as Oscar from *Angelique Trois* [GAME] started in 1998 and has 5 costumes

Sira Oscar Aota, 21 years old

Tsuyuha, 16 years old

as Kakashi Hatake from *Naruto* [MANGA] started in 2002 and has 5 costumes

This one calls to mind the splashy costumes of the all-female Takarazuka theater in Japan.

Fuga Serizawa

as Sasarai from *Genso Suikoden 3* [GAME] started in 1998 and has 20 costumes

A naughty boy magician, he summons demons to fight his battles.

as Ascot from *Magic Knight Rayearth* [ANIMATION] started in 1999 and has 15 costumes

Hinaki, 18 years old

Mari Kazukoshi

as Nanami Nono from *Hurricanger* [TELEVISION] started in 1996 and has many costumes

as a hero from *Tokyo Majin High School Gehocho* [GAME] started in 1997 and has 50 costumes

Jyaou Yagami

Cosplay Girls

Action Heroes

Sakura Himemiya, 24 years old

Don't let the pep squad smile fool you—she battles giant robots.

as Karin Son from *Voltage Fighter Gowcaizer* [GAME]

Youko Kagami, 21 years old

as Tina Branford from *Final Fantasy 6* [GAME] started in 1999 and has 15 costumes

Ryuta, 22 years old

as Eagle from *Magic Knight Rayearth* [ANIMATION] started in 2001 and has 3 costumes

Some pieces, like armor, are easier to buy than to make, if you have the cash.

Sai

as Tsugiri from *Alichino* [MANGA] started in 1995 and has 15 costumes

Zun, 22 years old

as Daishi from *Psycho le Cemu* [MUSIC] started in 1995 and has 15 costumes

Cosplay Girls 16

Kinoko, 23 years old

The Egyptian priest is a past-life incarnation of the comic's antagonist.

as Priest Seto from *Yu-Gi-Oh!* [MANGA] started in 2000 and has 20 costumes

Aya Kiryu

Bound and spiked, a young woman becomes a fetching pharaoh.

as Falao Yugi from *Yu-Gi-Oh!* [MANGA] started in 2000 and has 20 costumes

Kaname Anjyo

The original carries a sword, but she chooses to pack heat.

as Lagna Loire from *Final Fantasy 8* [GAME] started in 2001 and has 2 or 3 costumes

Suzuka Itsuki, 20 years old

as Sasuke Uchiha from *Naruto* [MANGA] started in 1999 and has 20 costumes

Action Heroes

Mia Fujikura, 20 years old

Kiyu, 24 years old

Souji Tamanegi 18 years old,

as Sasarai from *Genso Suikoden 3* [GAME] started in 2001 and has 8 costumes

One wonders if she can actually lift that gigantic sword.

as Kohaku from *Inuyasha* [ANIMATION]

as Cammy from *Street Fighter 2* [GAME] started in 1997 and has 10 costumes

as Fu Hououji from *Magic Knight Rayearth* [ANIMATION] started in 1998 and has 10 costumes

Karin Nonone, 22 years old

An oldie, but a goody. Part aerobics instructor, part Che Guevara, this look has been popular for about a decade.

Cosplay Girls   18

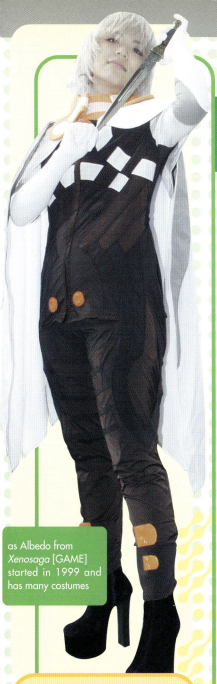

Hakone Tohyama, 19 years old

as Albedo from *Xenosaga* [GAME] started in 1999 and has many costumes

Platforms and a dagger make for a mix of medieval and mod here.

Rin, 24 years old

as Lock Cole from *Final Fantasy 6* [GAME] started in 1998 and has 20 costumes

Kuroko, 17 years old

as Kan-nei from *Shin Sangoku-musou* [GAME] started in 2000 and has 3 costumes

Airi

She's also defending the earth, but in snazzy blue.

as Umi Ryuuzaki from *Magic Knight Rayearth* [ANIMATION]

19 **Cosplay Girls**

COSPLAY RUNWAY
School Spirit

Since most Japanese students wear uniforms, cosplayers head back to school in neckties and pleated skirts. Lolita style (dressing as a young girl) is of course big.

In various states of messiness, these boy's uniforms are realistic.

Kiriha, 23 years old

Natsume Mayuki, 20 years old

Ren Hisui, 23 years old

from *Tokimeki Memorial: Girl's Side* [GAME]

Tamaki Asami as Yuki Souma from *Fruit Basket* [ANIMATION] started in 1994 and has 20 costumes

Kana, 17 years old

as Kisa Souma from *Fruit Basket* [ANIMATION] started in 2000 and has 7 costumes

as Rukia Kuchiki from *Bleach* [MANGA] started in 2001 and has 3 costumes

A little eerie how much she looks like a manga drawing.

Karin, 19 years old

Kokoa, 19 years old

as a hero from *Tokimeki Memorial: Girl's Side* [GAME] started in 2001 and has 3 costumes

as Kei Hazuki from *Tokimeki Memorial: Girl's Side* [GAME] started in 2002 and has 10 costumes

Mio Asakura, 22 years old

Anna

Cosplayers take the baby-doll look disturbingly far.

as Tomoyo Daidouji from *Card Captor Sakura* [ANIMATION] started in 2001 and has 6 costumes

Zeroshikigami

as Sakaki from *Azumanga Daioh* [ANIMATION] started in 1999

Asako, 18 years old

as Akemi from *Mr. Fullswing* [MANGA] started in 2001 and has 4 costumes

Takeshi Gouda

as Rei Ayanami from *Neon Genesis Evangelion* [ANIMATION]

21 Cosplay Girls

School Spirit

Yukira, 18 years old

Still in school, she probably wears something similar every day.

as Toru Honda from *Fruit Basket* [ANIMATION] started in 2002 and has 2 costumes

as Toru Honda from *Fruit Basket* [ANIMATION] since 2002 and has 1 costumes

Shuji, 21 years old

Noramikeneko, 22years old

Kani, 19 years old

from *Prince of Tennis* [ANIMATION]

Iori, 23 years old

as Rio Umeda from *Hanazakari No Kimitachi E* [MANGA] started in 1998 and has 20 costumes

This movie has school kids killing each other, which caused an uproar in Japan.

as Yukie Utsumi from *Battle Royale* [MOVIE] started in 2001 and has many costumes

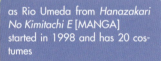

Seren Yurikawa, 23 years old

Cosplay Girls 22

COSPLAY RUNWAY
Sweet Things

These costume confections are whipped up with ribbons and bows for the ultimate in kawaii. Are your teeth aching yet?

Manyoh

as Bridget from *Guilty Gear XX* [GAME]

A popular gender-bender—she's dressed as a boy who is raised as a girl.

Kamiyu, 19 years old

as Hazuki Fuziwara from *Ojamajo Doremi* [ANIMATION] started in 1999 and has 15 costumes

Satomi, 21 years old

Some might say rubber and suspenders are a bit much, but they're not game designers.

as Tifa Lockheart from *Final Fantasy 7* [GAME] started in 1998 and has 10 costumes

Minami Marunouchi, 23 years old

as Olivia from *Grow Lanser 2* [GAME] started in 1997 and has 10 costumes

Yuri Hanamura
Yui Tohno
Yuka Ayamori

This trio blurs the line between prince & princess.

Cosplay Girls

Sweet Things

Kou Kiyono

as Chosen from *Shin Sangoku-musou 2* [GAME]

as Meroko from *Full Moon wo Sagashite* started in 2000 and has 5 costumes

This character is an angel of Death, bit the fluffy costume takes some of the sting out of it.

Yuki, 20 years old

A computer in pigtails, but with a Gothic Lolita touch.

Mahru, 20 years old

as Emilou from *La Reine* [MUSIC] started in 2000 and has 20 costumes

as Chii from *Chobits* [MANGA] started in 2002 and has 1 costume

Ayano Tsukishiro

Saki

as Sumomo from *Chobits* [ANIMATION] started in 1996 and has 50 costumes

Hyuga, 21 years old

as May from *Guilty Gear XX* [GAME] started in 1998 and has 7 costumes

Kokoa, 19 years old

as Poet from *Pop'n Music* [GAME] started in 2001 and has 3 costumes

Himari Fukamachi, 21 years old

It's enough to send a person into insulin shock.

as Sugar from *Tiny Snow Fairy Sugar* [ANIMATION]

Sana, 17 years old

as April from *Guilty Gear XX* [GAME] started in 1998 and has 10 costumes

Kaori Kisui, 23 years old

as Sakura Kinomoto from *Card Captor Sakura* [ANIMATION] started in 1996 and has many costumes

She looks lile a cutie, but she's a little witch.

Kotono Nagase, 21 years old

as Sailor Moon from *Sailor Moon* [ANIMATION] started in 1999 and has 4 costumes

Cosplay Girls

Sweet Things

Yomomi
as Sailor Mercury from *Sailor Moon* [ANIMATION] has 5 costumes

Another school girl out to save the world.

Hironamin-C, 21 years old
as Momoko Asuka from *Ojamajo Doremi* [ANIMATION] started in 1998 and has 20 costumes

Ichigo Yukikura, 19 years old
as Sayaka Takai from *Welcome to Pia Carrot Vol.3* [GAME] started in 2001 and has 10 costumes

Mizuki, 16 years old
as Bridget from *Guilty Gear XX* [GAME] started in 2001 and has 5 costumes

Despite the porn-ish title, it's pretty innocent stuff.

Rokuya, 22 years old
as Chii from *Chobits* [ANIMATION] started in 1993 and has 40 costumes

Shirou, 20 years old
as Mikado Ushio from *Mr. Fullswing* [MANGA] started in 2000

Chiro, 19 years old
as Akemi from *Mr. Fullswing* [MANGA] started in 2001 and has 10 costumes

Cosplay Girls 26

Aya Matsushima, 24 years old

as a maid [ORIGINAL] started in 1996 and has 40 costumes

Ayata, 6 years old

as Kiki from *Kiki's Delivery Service* [ANIMATION] started in 1998

Kotone Katakura

as Rinoa Heartilly from *Final Fantasy 8* [GAME] started in 2001 and has 7 costumes

Almost lifelike, isn't she?

Chippy

This magical youngster could give the flying nun a run for her money.

as Doremi Harukaze from *Ojamajo Doremi* [ANIMATION] started in 2002 and has 4 costumes

Aika, 20 years old

as Sailor Pluto from *Sailor Moon* [ANIMATION] started in 2001 and has 30 costumes

Sagiri

as Amami Hasegawa from *Welcome to Pia Carrot Vol.3* [GAME] started in 2001 and has 8 costumes

Sweet Things

Yuzuru

as Doremi Harukaze from *Ojamajo Doremi* [ANIMATION] started in 2001 and has 20 costumes

The shoes and broom make this pink witch ensemble.

Manaki

as Princess [ORIGINAL] started in 1993 and has many costumes

Haru, 22 years old

This show has inspired Japanese school girls to roll their skirts into scandalous minis.

as Sailor Uranus from *Sailor Moon* [ANIMATION] started in 2001 and has 10 costumes

Kairi Seto, 22 years old

as Yuzuki from *Chobits* [ANIMATION] started in 1998 and has many costumes

Izumi

as Sailor Jupiter from *Sailor Moon* [ANIMATION] started in 2001 and has 10 costumes

Cosplay Girls

Miyuki Mizui, 18 years old

The pigeon-toed slouch is supposed to be the height of cuteness.

as Aya from *Psycho le Cemu* [MUSIC] started in 1999 and has 60 costumes

as Angelique Limoges from *Angelique Special 2* [GAME] started in 2001 and has 30 costumes

Culai

Kamome Hourou, 24 years old

Shian, 22 years old

as Chii from *Chobits* [ANIMATION] started in 2001 and has 10 costumes

as Chii from *Chobits* [ANIMATION] started in 1998 and has 5 costumes

Riko Yatsuhashi, 17 years old

The love of waitress outfits is puzzling in a country with no tipping.

as Lettuce Midorikawa from *Tokyo Mew Mew* [ANIMATION] started in 2001 and has 3 costumes

as Misha from *Pita-ten* [ANIMATION] started in 1995 and has 10 costumes

Yu Saeki, 23 years old

Tsuaki, 20 years old

as Aya from *Psycho le Cemu* [MUSIC] started in 1998 and has 10 costumes

Cosplay Girls

Sweet Things

Sakana Noru, 9 years old

This little pirate's tuckered-out from a day of cosplay.

as May from *Guilty Gear XX* [GAME] started in 2001 and has 6 costumes

from *Sailor Moon* [ANIMATION]

Otoko Innami, 20 years old

as Anthy Himemiya from *Revolutionary Girl Utena* [ANIMATION] started in 2001 and has 8 costumes

Tsubasa, 25 years old

as Nami from *One Piece* [ANIMATION] started in 1996 and has 15 costumes

Eruru, 17 years old

as Milfeulle Sakuraba from *Galaxy Angel* [ANIMATION] started in 2000 and has 12 costumes

Cosplay Girls

COSPLAY RUNWAY
Sci Fi

Cyber-chic is big on the cosplay scene, especially with so many robot and cyborg characters to choose from.

Sono

as Rei Ayanami from *Neon Genesis Evangelion* [ANIMATION] started in 2000 and has 10 costumes

Chiharu Kannagi

as A-S Signal from *Twin Signal* [ANIMATION] started in 1992 and has many costumes

Zakuro, 19 years old

as a Ground Examination Team member from *Pure Trance* [MANGA] started in 1999 and has 10 costumes

Amehiko Sato, 19 years old

as Albert Heinrich from *Cyborg 009* [ANIMATION] started in 1992 and has 20 costumes

Susumu Nakano, 18 years old

as Joe Shimamura from *Cyborg 009* [ANIMATION] started in 1995 and has 20 costumes

There's something very Wonder Twins about this duo with their bobs and boots.

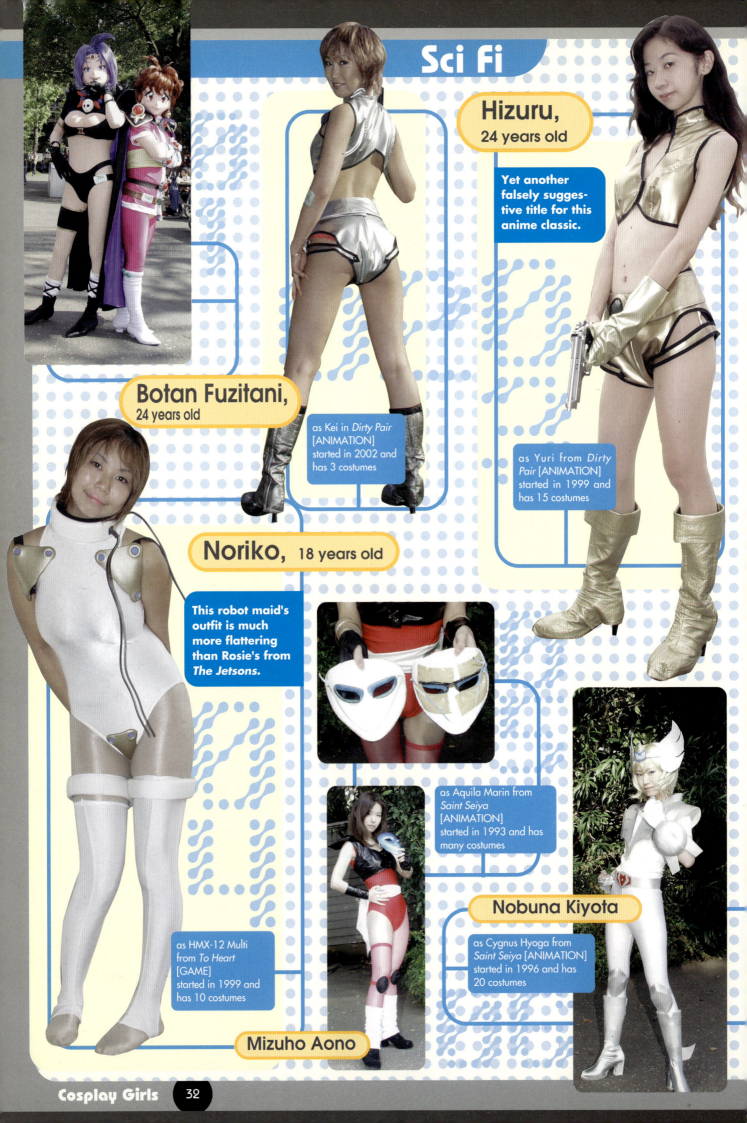

Sci Fi

Hizuru, 24 years old

Yet another falsely suggestive title for this anime classic.

as Yuri from *Dirty Pair* [ANIMATION] started in 1999 and has 15 costumes

Botan Fuzitani, 24 years old

as Kei in *Dirty Pair* [ANIMATION] started in 2002 and has 3 costumes

Noriko, 18 years old

This robot maid's outfit is much more flattering than Rosie's from *The Jetsons*.

as HMX-12 Multi from *To Heart* [GAME] started in 1999 and has 10 costumes

Mizuho Aono

as Aquila Marin from *Saint Seiya* [ANIMATION] started in 1993 and has many costumes

Nobuna Kiyota

as Cygnus Hyoga from *Saint Seiya* [ANIMATION] started in 1996 and has 20 costumes

Cosplay Girls 32

Some cosplayers are devoted to a single character, like the animated Cutie Honey. Others pride themselves on their wide range of costumes.

Special thanks to Brazilian Music&Jazz Bar DUO

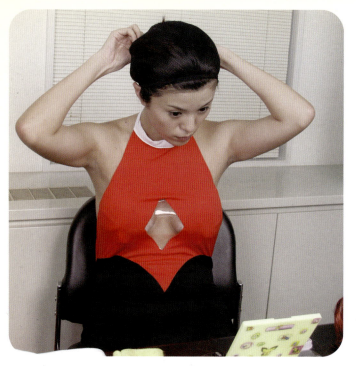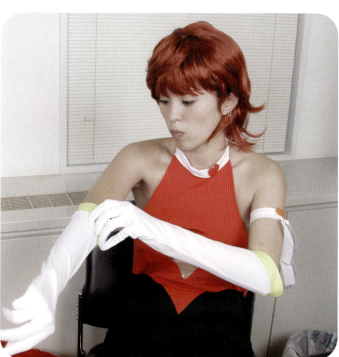

Transformation

COSPLAY RUNWAY
Animal Kingdom

Four-legged characters are wildly popular and so are their cuddly costumes.

Rei, 19 years old

as Karumaramon from *Digimon Frontier* [ANIMATION] started in 1997 and has 50 costumes

Yuki, 22 years old

as Ichigo Momomiya from *Tokyo Mew Mew* [ANIMATION] started in 2000 and has 6 costumes

Momono

Looking devilish as a vinyl version of the tiny monster.

Rino Minazuki, 24 years old

as Juri from *Yu Yu Hakusho* [ANIMATION] started in 1997 and has 15 costumes

Satome, 22 years old

as Guilmon from *Digimon Tamers* [ANIMATION] started in 1999 and has 20 costumes

as Renamon from *Digimon Tamers* [ANIMATION] started in 1999 and has 4 costumes

The mike isn't for karaoke, she's a ringside referee.

39 Cosplay Girls

Animal Kingdom

Mariko Iimura, 20 years old

You just can't go wrong adding ears and a tail to an outfit.

Kanoe, 25 years old

as Pyokola Analogue III from *Di Gi Charat* [ANIMATION] started in 1997 and has 15 costumes

Miho Nakajima, 27 years old

as Cat Girl [ORIGINAL] started in 1993 and has 50 costumes

as Ichigo Momomiya from *Tokyo Mew Mew* [ANIMATION] started in 2000 and has 5 costumes

Beniko Kiryu, 19 years old

as Mew Mint from *Tokyo Mew Mew* [ANIMATION] started in 2001 and has 8 costumes

Moko Sakuno, 19 years old

as Ichigo Momomiya from *Tokyo Mew Mew* [ANIMATION] started in 2002 and has 20 costumes

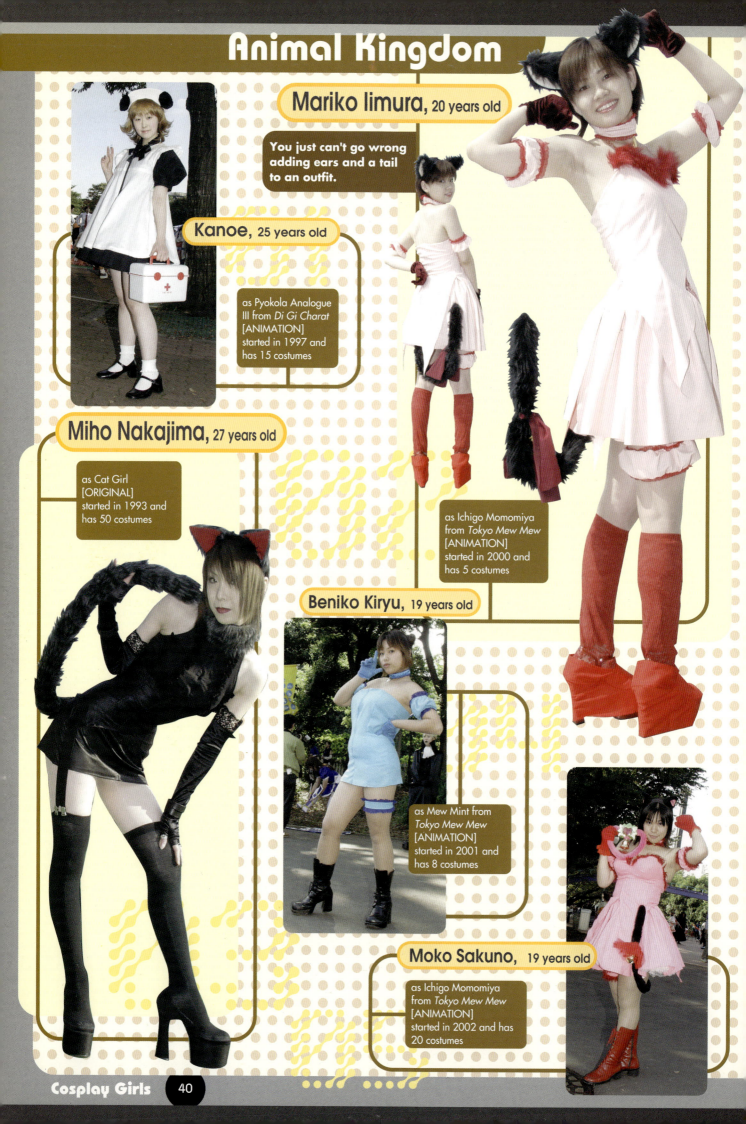

Yukie, 19 years old

Believe it or not, this March Hare/ can-can girl is supposed to be a kind of Grim Reaper.

as Meroko from *Full Moon wo Sagashite* [ANIMATION] started in 1999 and has 5 costumes

Shiki, 23 years old

as Syutsumon from *Digimon Frontier* [ANIMATION]

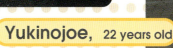

Yukinojoe, 22 years old

as Hikaru Usada from *Di Gi Charat* [ANIMATION] started in 1995 and has 10 costumes

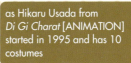

Ranfa

as Dizzy from *Guilty Gear XX* [GAME] started in 1995 and has 10 costumes

Shogo Kageo, 24 years old

as the Cheshire Cat from *Alice's Adventures in Wonderland* [NOVEL] started in 1995 and has 10 costumes

Animal Kingdom

Hideki
as Rik Heisenberg from *Di Gi Charat* [ANIMATION] started in 1999 and has 15 costumes

Kaoru, 20 years old
as Dejiko from *Di Gi Charat* [ANIMATION] started in 2000 and has 10 costumes

Kururun, 8 years old
as Misya from *Pita-ten* [ANIMATION] started in 1997 and has 8 costumes

Satomi Morisawa
as Zakuro Fuziwara from *Tokyo Mew Mew* [ANIMATION] started in 1995 and has 10 costumes

Masaki, 21 years old
as Kyubimon from *Digimon Tamers* [ANIMATION] started in 2001 and has 10 costumes

The fur tube top and leg warmers are a unique interpretation of this well-known reindeer character.

Arisa Kurano
as Tony Tony Chopper from *One Piece* [MANGA] started in 1996 and has 50 costumes

Cosplay Girls 42

Machi, 22 years old

as Koto from *Yu Yu Hakusho* [ANIMATION] started in 1997 and has 7 costumes

Tairou Yamada, 18 years old

as Patamon from *Digimon Frontier* [ANIMATION]

Mayuko, 22 years old

as Merchant from *Ragnarok Online* [GAME] started in 1995 and has 30 costumes

Yuzu, Ichigo, Momo, Anzu, Ringo

as Ichigo, Pudding, Lettuce, Mint, Zakuro, from *Tokyo Mew Mew* [ANIMATION]

Hitomi Arakawa, 24 years old

as Erica Fontaine from *Sakura Wars 3* [GAME] started in 2002 and has 1 costume

COSPLAY RUNWAY
Gothic & Lolita

This look is a scary cocktail of Goth/Vampire fashion and the Japanese fascination with girlhood innocence. The standard is a lacy black and white maid's outfit, but color sometimes enters the mix.

Haru, 23 years old

The furry ears take this from a standard goth outfit to a cosplay classic.

as Smile from *Pop'n Music* [GAME] started in 1999 and has 10 costumes

Enjyu

Miho Takehara, 22 years old

as Flower-Lolita [ORIGINAL] started in 1995 and has 4 costumes

as Ash from *Pop'n Music* [GAME] started in 1998 and has 10 costumes

Bibi, 19 years old

as Smile from *Pop'n Music* [GAME] started in 2002 and has 6 costumes

Cosplay Girls 44

Miya Akatuki, 19 years old

as Hajime Saitou from *Rurouni Kenshin* [ANIMATION] started in 2000 and has 5 costumes

Ao Kiriha

as Yuri from *Pop'n Music* [GAME] started in 2002 and has 7 costumes

Ranka

Garters and bonnets are de rigueur for this creepy Little Bo-Peep style.

In Gothic & Lolita style [Original] started in 2001 and has 3 costumes

Manaka

as Mana from *Malice Mizer* [MUSIC] started in 1999 and has 10 costumes

45 Cosplay Girls

Gothic & Lolita

Looks like Little Red Riding Hood fell in with a bad crowd.

Sachi Kashimura, 20 years old

As Bulleta from *Vampire Savior* [GAME] started in 1996

Yasuko Aizawa, 36 years old

Karin, 19 years old

in "Lolita" style [ORIGINAL] started in 2002 and has 6 costumes

Plenty of music groups have elaborate costumes imitated by fans. KISS, anyone?

as Mana from *Malice Mizer* [MUSIC] started in 2001 and has 10 costumes

Fran, 30 years old

as De Dood from *Elisabeth* [MUSICAL] started in 1997 and has 10 costumes

Sei, 20 years old

as Kyo from *Dir en Grey* [MUSIC] started in 2000 and has 10 costumes

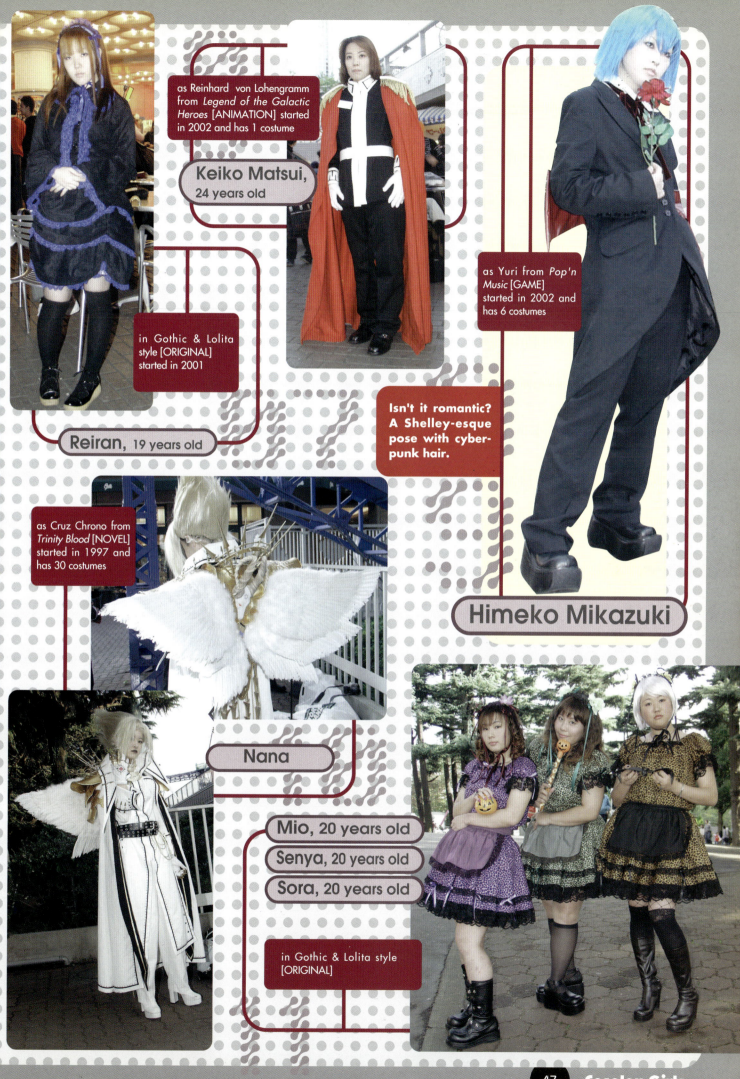

Plenty of cosplayers would love to spend every day in costume. Of course, letting your boss know you dress like a tiny cartoon angel on weekends isn't always the best idea. So most cosplayers are in the closet at the office.

9-5

At 500 yen (about $4.20), the Melon Float is a popular menu item, and darn cute. Prices are pretty much the same as other coffee shops.

Cosplay Coffee Shop
Mai:lish

[FH Kyowa Square 2F, 3-6-2,
Soto-Kanda, Chiyoda-ku, Tokyo
Tel 03-5289-7310
Open daily, 11:00AM - 10:00PM]

On Meganekko (Kids with Glasses) Day, nobody gets in without a pair of specs on, staff and customers alike. Yukata Day, when everyone dons traditional summer kimono, and Sports Day, when everyone dresses as athletes or cheerleaders, are also sights to see.

Since Mai:lish opened in 2002, work clothes have meant anything from animal suits to video game and anime costumes. When "Maid Time" finishes at 5:00pm, the seven waitresses exchange their frilly aprons for something more their style. The charms of cosplay attire haven't gone unnoticed by the mostly male clientele, who time their visits according to the girls' shifts, and will even honor their favorite waitresses with flowers on their birthdays. Their loyalty is rewarded each Wednesday, when Mai:lish holds its special events day.

Waitress character collectibles, badges, and telephone cards are on sale at the entrance.

Between them, the waitresses own upwards of 100 costumes!

Although most customers are men in their twenties and thirties, more and more cosplayer women are discovering Mai:lish.

Cosplay Girls 52

COSPLAY RUNWAY
Asian Style

Japanese and Chinese traditional clothing are tossed in the blender with elements of Sci-Fi and Glam. The result is a kind of pan-Asian costume fusion.

Sera, 20 years old

This dreamy high school heroine was transported from her real life to a fantasy world. You can see the appeal.

as Yoko Nakajima from *The Twelve Kingdoms* [ANIMATION] started in 2000 and has 10 costumes

as Montenmaru from *Tokyo Majin High School Gehocho* [GAME] started in 2002 and has 7 costumes

Kisaragi, 23 years old

as Kenshin Himura from *Rurouni Kenshin* [ANIMATION] started in 1999

Ayara, 20 years old

as Shampoo from *Ranma 1/2* [ANIMATION] started in 1995 and has 10 costumes

Hokuto, 20 years old

Yuzu, 20 years old

as Kikyo from *Tokyo Majin High School* [GAME] started in 1997 and has 10 costumes

Cosplay Girls

Asian Style

Kaguya Hibiki, 20 years old

Maya
as Shibai from *Shin Sangoku-musou 2* [GAME] started in 2002

Her fans are deadly weapons in the game, but threaten with only paper cuts here.

as Mai Shiranui from *King of Fighters* [GAME] started in 1998 and has 20 costumes

Kakeru, 21 years old

The boy side-kick to the heroine is decked out in simpler chinoiserie.

as Rokuta from *The Twelve Kingdoms* [ANIMATION] started in 1997 and has 10 costumes

as Yuki Souma from *Fruit Basket* [ANIMATION] started in 2000 and has 10 costumes

Chiharu Yogiri, 17 years old

from *Shin Sangoku-musou 2* [GAME]

Hinatsu Momose, 20 years old
Rin Kujou, 20 years old

Yukino, 20 years old

Another fighter ready to rumble in ribbons.

as Kasumi from *Dead or Alive 3* [GAME]

Hinaki, 18 years old

from *Hikaru No Go ~Heian Gensou Ibunroku~* [GAME]

Ryuuta, 22 years old

Subaru Hyuga, 21 years old

as Hisui from *Haruka Naru Toki No Naka De 2* [GAME] started in 2002 and has 3 costumes

as Sang-Yun from *Magic Knight Rayearth 2* [ANIMATION] started in 1997 and has 40 costumes

Haruki Sakuragi, 20 years old

Kaito, 16 years old

as Kaoru Kamiya from *Rurouni Kenshin* [ANIMATION] started in 2002 and has 4 costumes

A servant boy's costume is topped off with a Chinese beanie.

Cosplay

Rikyu, 19 years old

This vestal virgin costume is pretty faithful to the Shinto original.

as a Shrine maiden [ORIGINAL] started in 1999 and has 10 costumes

Hotaru Hoshino, 15 years old

as Soushi Okita from Shinsengumi [HISTORY] started in 2000 and has 10 costumes

as Misono Fuziwarano from *Haruka Naru Toki No Naka De 2* [GAME] started in 2000 and has 8 costumes

Yuki, 19 years old

Mine, 18 years old

as Momizi Souma from *Fruit Basket* [ANIMATION] started in 2002 and has 7 costumes

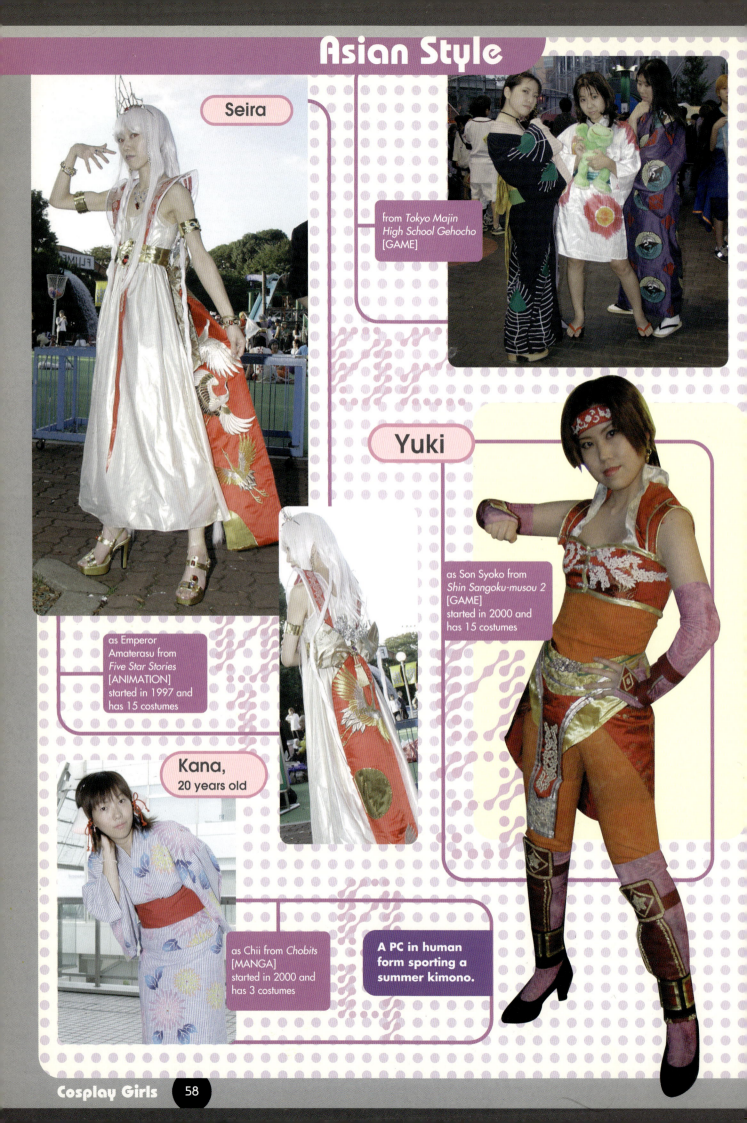

Takeo, 19 years old

as Sakura Haruno from *Naruto* [MANGA] started in 1995 and has 10 costumes

A female ninja novice, but with a lot more fashion flair than the traditional dark suited spies.

Asakura, 20 years old

as Syu-yu from *Shin Sangoku-musou* [GAME] started in 2002 and has 2 costumes

Mayuka Koga

as Yuna from *Final Fantasy 10* [GAME] started in 1998 and has 20 costumes

as Hyo from *Tokyo Majin High School* [GAME] started in 1997 and has 10 costumes

Touko, 20 years old

from *Shin Sangoku-musou* [GAME]

Sei Kyou, 22 years old

En, 19 years old

Cosplay Girls

COSPLAY RUNWAY
Pin-up Girls

The women of anime, games, and manga are often drawn with proportions that would make Varga gasp. But even mortal women can sample the fantasy with a teeny bikini and a pout.

Eru Amamiya

as Chii from *Chobits* [MANGA] started in 1995 and has 50 costumes

She's one of many humanoid computer characters, but in Lolita cheesecake style.

Yuki, 18 years old

from *Angel Sanctuary* [MANGA]

Noriko Yurugi, 18 years old

Kurara

as Sofia from *Toushinden* [GAME] started in 1998 and has 10 costumes

With bat wings fluttering in her hair, she wields magic against her opponents.

as Morrigan from *Vampire Savior* [GAME] started in 1996 and has 6 costumes

Saori Shimizu, 20 years old

Cosplay Girls 60

Momo, 21 years old

This calendar girl look may seem a little easy, but it takes dedication in the winter.

as Bikini [Original] started in 1996 and has 6 costumes

Fuminyanko, 27 years old

as Dizzy from *Guilty Gear XX* [GAME] started in 1992 and has 15 costumes

Kaori

as I-no from *Guilty Gear XX* [GAME] started in 1999 and has 20 costumes

as Rei Ayanami from *Neon Genesis Evangelion* [ANIMATION] started in 1996 and has 50 costumes

She may look like a pin-up girl, but her character pilots a robot and battles alien invaders.

Ran

A real cat-fighter, the fur flies when she gets in the ring with other creatures from this game.

Ai Haruna

as Felicia in *Vampire Savior* [GAME] started in 1996 and has 30 costumes

Cosplay Girls

Fantasy and Sci-Fi characters, like robot pilot Rei Ayanami, often call for elaborate costumes, wigs, props, and make-up. Some cosplayers like a challenge-- and everybody likes a space suit.

REI AYANAMI

Kamen Rider Amazon Figurine

Cosplay Boutique
OLIVE AKIHABARA

Toda Bldg 4F, 1-3-10
Soto-Kanda, Chiyoda-ku, Tokyo
Tel: 03-5256-0010
Open daily, 11:30AM - 10:00PM

A helmet sells for 240,000 yen (around $2,000).

This mask goes for 180,000 yen (around $1,500).

There's no mistaking Olive's specialty. Located in Tokyo's cosplay mecca, Akihabara, Olive's walls are covered in costumes of every variety, from anime to uniforms. A production staff is on hand to deal with orders, and will consider even the most outlandish designs and models. But nothing here comes cheap. In the cosplay world, 50,000 yen (around $420) is a small price to pay. There's no limit to how much the truly obsessed are willing to part with.

Kamen Rider Figurine

Olive's Top-Selling Three

After being measured, a customer discusses her budget and is given an estimate. Costumes take at least two to three weeks to make.

No.1 Welcome to Pia Carrot costume, 45,000 yen (around $380). An original design popular with both sexes.

A customer's order with hand-drawn outlines.

No.2 Chobits costume, 45,000 yen (around $380). Taken from the cult anime, it's simple but cute.

No.3 Tokyo Mew Mew costume, 50,000 yen (around $420). The rich satin gives it a luxurious look.

Kamen Rider V3 Figurine

Cosplay Girls

COSPLAY RUNWAY
Stranger Than Fashion

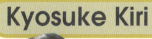

From classic characters to original creations, anything goes in cosplay. In fact, the wierder the better for some.

Kyosuke Kiri

as Sapphirus Hawthorne from *Apocripha/0* [GAME] started in 1998

The royal tutor strikes a scholarly pose.

as Abel Nightroad from *Trinity Blood* [NOVEL] started in 1997 and has 30 costumes

Ruka, 24 years old

as Etsuko Mita [PROFESSIONAL WRESTLING] started in 1997

Yosshi, 22 years old

Rei Kohinata, 22 years old

She didn't raid Elton John's closet- she actually made this from scratch.

as Miss America from *Battle Fever J* [ACTION HERO] started in 2000 and has 4 costumes

Miss America

as Myobi from *Alichino* [MANGA] started in 1999 and has 15 costumes

65 Cosplay Girls

Stranger Than Fashion

Yuhi, 22 years old

Numaty, 20 years old

as Mima Shimoda [PROFESSIONAL WRESTLING] started in 2002 and has 2 costumes

This one has a real club kid feel.

Yukari Chida, 28 years old

as Squalo from *Jojo's Bizarre Adventure* [MANGA] started in 2000 and has 10 costumes

Hit, 21 years old

as Augsta Vradica from *Trinity Blood* [NOVEL] started in 1993 and has 50 costumes

Prison drab but for the tiny panda pinned over her heart.

Nagisa Sakura, 29 years old

Kurosaura, 29 years old

as maids [ORIGINAL]

Nekodamao, 26 years old

as Pyocola Analogue III from *DiGi Charat* [ANIMATION]

as Fumiko Odette van Stein from *Shikigami No Shiro* [GAME] started in 1995 and has 30 costumes

Cosplay Girls 66

The Takarazuka-influenced story features women in romantic/Vegas versions of men's military dress uniforms.

as Utena Tenjou from *Revolutionary Girl Utena* [ANIMATION] started in 1996 and has 30 costumes

Rin Izumi, 22 years old

as Astharoshe Asran from *Trinity Blood* [NOVEL] started in 1997 and has 50 costumes

Aki

Yumira

as Caterina Sforza from *Trinity Blood* [NOVEL] started in 2000 and has 5 costumes

as Team Union Savior's campaign Girl from *Future GPX Cyber Formula* [ANIMATION]

Hiryu, 20 years old

as Skull from *Cyborg 009* [ANIMATION] started in 2002 and has 4 costumes

Yoshiko, 25 years old

as Astharoshe Asran from *Trinity Blood* [NOVEL] started in 1992 and has 20 costumes

Shiho, 23 years old

67 Cosplay Girls

Stranger Than Fashion

Yukako, 21 years old

as Helga Von Vogelweide from *Trinity Blood* [NOVEL]

Buns to rival Princess Leia's.

Mari Fukida

as Jenny from *Pokemon* [ANIMATION] started in 1998 and has 6 costumes

Toujyu

as Ion Fortuna from *Trinity Blood* [NOVEL] started in 1999 and has 10 costumes

Sawa

as Aisha from *Romancing SaGa* [GAME] started in 1993 and has 5 costumes

Mimi

as Barbara from *Romancing SaGa* [GAME] started in 1993 and has 5 costumes

Alumi

as Ulala from *Space Channel 5 Part 2* [GAME] started in 1999 and has 6 costumes

Cosplay Girls

The lightning throwing Princess Lum-chan is a perennial favorite.

as Lum from *Urusei Yatsura* [ANIMATION] started in 1998 and has 20 costumes

Kguya Hibiki, 20 years old

Abel, 21 years old

from *Cyborg 009* [ANIMATION]

as Benten from *Urusei Yatsura* [ANIMATION] started in 1998 and has 13 costumes

Shikimi Matsuzawa, 21 years old

Fumiko, 21 years old

Lum-chan's pal has an S&M look with her treasured chain accessory.

Seiichi Hayakawa, 21 years old

as Esther Blanchett from *Trinity Blood* [NOVEL] started in 1999 and has 7 costumes

Tareneko, 21 years old

Emiri, 23 years old

as Zizz from *Pop'n Music* [GAME] started in 1991 and has 6 costumes

as Team Missing Link's campaign girl from *Future GPX Cyber Formula* [ANIMATION] started in 1996 and has 20 costumes

69 **Cosplay Girls**

Stranger Than Fashion

Ready for the hunt in a blond wig and a mini.

Kouki Hijiri, 25 years old

as Julius from *Angelique* [GAME] started in 1999 and has 10 costumes

as Female Archer from *Ragnarok Online* [GAME] started in 2001 and has 10 costumes

Fujine Masaki

as Astharoshe Asran from *Trinity Blood* [NOVEL] started in 1990 and has 30 costumes

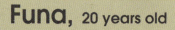

Funa, 20 years old

Makoto Higa, 19 years old

Merata, 20 years old

Shinon Oumi, 21 years old

Her giant feline friend is from a different game altogether.

as Erica Fontaine from *Sakura Wars 3* [GAME] started in 2002 and has 1 costume

Hiroko, 19 years old

From *Alice's Adventures in Wonderland* [NOVEL]

Misato, 19 years old
from *Shaman King* [ANIMATION]

Yuma, 18 years old

Eko, 17 years old

Aya, 27 years old
as Augsta Vradica from *Trinity Blood* [NOVEL] has 50 costumes

Kimi Shimizu, 16 years old
as Vivi from *Final Fantasy 9* [GAME] started in 2002 and has 1 costume

Karyou, 21 years old
The striped wig and foil-wrapped staff make this one special.
as Astharoshe Asran from *Trinity Blood* [NOVEL] started in 1997 and has 30 costumes

Ahiru Tachibana, 21 years old
Dressed in an event-staff uniform, her sign reads "End of the Line."
as Minami Makimura from *Comic Party* [GAME] started in 2001 and has 8 costumes

Cosplay Girls

Backstage

COSPLAYERS AT HOME

Too many costumes to count!

**Sakura Himemiya (24)
Cosplay career: 11 years**

Attended her first event at the age of 13. Made her cosplay debut at 15. Since then she has worked part-time to support her cosplayer lifestyle.

Her closet is filled with costumes, none of which can be washed.

Sakura has the whole set of *Yu Yu Hakusho* manga, her inspiration during her junior high school days.

Cosplay accessories. The satchel belongs to a friend's younger sister. The black schoolbag Sakura bought herself.

Her room usually looks like this. The big teddy bear has probably seen a few cosplay events as a prop.

Probably the one incident I remember most happened at a summer event. I had just turned 15. In fact, it's become kind of a legend now. I went as Mami Shimura's android from the game *KasaGyo*. Back then, cameko didn't have to line up like they do now. Although they used to kind of surround you, they still could only take pictures from the front. Back and side shots still aren't allowed. But on that day there were so many of them - all around me all I could see were cameko. The staff tried to do something about it, but somehow couldn't get them to stop. I couldn't even begin to count how many cameras there were. There were just so many. What are they all so interested in, I kept thinking. I was really panicking.

I've appeared as a cosplayer in the magazine *Asian Freak* about three times. I've also been in porno magazines quite a few times. Do I get angry with cameko for sending my photos to magazines like that? I don't really think about it. It's not like

I'm revealing my body or showing my underwear or anything. There's nothing to be ashamed about. Still, I'm a bit embarrassed about everyone seeing me doing cosplay. I do it because I like it, but I can't control what happens to the photos people take of me. There have been thousands taken. Since I started I've never really minded.

I used to keep a list of all the costumes I made, but after making my 200th costume I gave up counting. It made me realize how cosplay has taken over my life. As soon as I save a bit of money I spend it. Actually, my grandmother made me my first costume. I showed her a book and told her what had to be done, and she made it by the next day! I got her to make costumes for all my friends as well. She didn't like me doing cosplay but she went ahead and made them even as she was complaining. After that, she taught me how to sew, and now I make all my own stuff.

I used to say that I would quit once I turned 20. But I'm already 24! Most of my friends from that time have stopped. But I couldn't be happy without cosplay. It's not like I'm using it to escape from reality or anything. I'm like everyone else. Sure, when I started everyone was a bit surprised, but I'm just an ordinary girl. It's not like I don't have a boyfriend or anything.

I'm off to Osaka and Fukuoka soon. Of course, I'm going to some cosplay events.

PHOTO MEMORIES

The cosplay legend! Back when Sakura was just a schoolgirl.

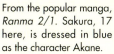

From the popular manga, *Ranma 2/1*. Sakura, 17 here, is dressed in blue as the character Akane.

From the game *Idol Project*, popular in Sakura's teens. She's on the right. The other cosplayer is a boy.

18 year-old Sakura is on the left, kneeling. She even made the feathers herself.

Sakura at 20, on the right, sitting. Her character is Atena from the game *King of Fighters*.

Halloween party. With her navel out, 19 year-old Sakura suddenly looks grown-up.

Sakura's cosplay photo collection. Altogether there are 25 albums, a lifetime's worth.

Grandmother Kimiko. It can't be easy having a cosplayer granddaughter.

Cosplay Girls

COSPLAYERS AT HOME

I Could Never Live with Someone Who Wasn't a Cosplayer!

Kimie Kuwana (20)
Cosplay career: 4 Years
Miyuki Munakata (20)
Cosplay career: 4 Years

Friends since junior high school, Kimie and Myuki got into cosplay when they were 16. Today they share an apartment just outside Tokyo.

Both are big *Pokemon* fans. They've even got collectors items from the opening of the New York Pokemon Center. Between them they reckon they've spent over 200,000 yen (about $1,700) on *Pokemon* alone! Obsessed?

They each have over 1,000 *Pokemon* cards. Enough to impress even American kids!

Costumes that they've made together. Some they've thrown away, others they've given to friends.

Kimie Kuwana: Why cosplay? I suppose it's because I love the characters in manga and anime. When I love a character, I want to become it! I guess that's how I got into it.

Miyuki Munakata: In junior high school we used to go to cosplay events all the time, didn't we?

KK: Our lifestyle is totally different from other people. If we want to buy material, we cut back on food and other living expenses. When I'm buying shoes or clothes, I always worry whether or not I can use them with my costumes. I'm also on a diet most of the time.

MM: If we put on weight the other cosplayers won't think much of us. Even our friends. But we hate it, too, when there's someone trying to be the same character as us but looking lame.

KK: Everyone has the same attitude, so we have to think about it as well. Also, we've got to have our weekends free. Where we both work, we get Saturdays and Sundays off. But that's why there are so many cosplayers doing part time work. Or government jobs.

MM: A third of my salary goes toward cosplay. Together we've spent well over 500,000 yen (about $3,500).

Cosplay Girls

KK: Almost every weekend we're at a cosplay event. Maybe about eight times a month. If there's no event, we stay in and make costumes.

MM: That's why neither of us can imagine living with anyone who isn't a cosplayer. We're together all the time - at work, after work, on days off - but we don't care. We never fight. It's fun to do stuff together because we're both really into cosplay.

KK: At the company where we work we keep it all a secret. I don't think there are any other cosplayers there.

MM: We can always tell when we talk to someone if they're into it or not.

KK: We make all our own costumes now. When we started we used to buy them. We just didn't think we could make anything. But because I've studied some Japanese and Western dressmaking, I thought we might as well give it a shot.

MM: My costumes are always made on an impulse. I'll just try it, I think. Or I want to see what something would look like. Sometimes I even make five or six in one month. That's when there's a big event or when I want to have something new. If we work together, it takes us from half to a whole day to finish one piece.

KK: It was great when we were at an event wearing our own stuff and people shouted out the characters' names to us. It was like we were really being recognized.

MM: I was twice as pleased because I'd made both the costumes. When that happened I really got the feeling that everything we'd done had been worthwhile.

KK: We've made loads of friends.

MM: We've got more than 100 cosplayer friends all over Japan. We meet people at events and on-line from as far north as Sendai right down to Fukuoka in the south.

Kimie's room is decorated mostly with her *Pokemon* collection and posters.

The women's wigs. Kimie also colors her hair to make cosplay easier.

The secret of hairpiece success? Stick a bathing cap on first! The wig won't budge now.

Before putting the wig on, fasten the cap with a few hairpins. That'll keep the whole thing on.

The perfect piece for hours of hard-core cosplay partying.

Costumes are worked on as a team. Kimie sketches characters from video.

By following the sketches, Myuki puts the costumes together. Here's their trusty sewing machine and some pieces from their fabric collection.

Myuki's the one with dressmaking skills. Kimie's in charge of accessories.

Myuki's room has a feminine feel, with tatami mats on the floor and all her favorite manga comics on the bookshelves.

Cosplay Girls

Do It Yourself: Cosplay Couture

Half the fun of cosplay can be making your own costume. Ready-made is fine, but there's a real satisfaction in wearing something you've put real effort into. These simple instructions show you just how they do it. Why not give it a try?

1 Research

Go to the source. Raid books, video, and the Internet for images of your character.

2 Take Notes

Keep a running list of important points, such as measurements, etc. You might also include a rough sketch of the finished design.

3 Required Tools

Sewing machine, needles, scissors, ruler, measuring tape, chalk marker, fabric glue, iron, thimble, etc.

4 Measuring Yourself

Take measurements of your shoulders, arm lengths, bust, waist, hips, thighs, etc.

5 Choosing the Material

The feel of the material, its price, color, and availability; choose wisely, as these can make or break your costume and your budget. This is a chance to really put your imagination to work.

6 Bits & Pieces

At the same time, prepare the extras, like cord, Velcro, zippers, hooks, ribbon, etc.

7 Patterns

You can either buy patterns, or make your own from ordinary paper. Always make your own patterns a little larger than the finished size to allow for seams.

8 Marking Out the Fabric

Place the paper patterns onto the fabric and very carefully stencil the outline around each with the chalk marker.

9 Cutting the Fabric

Now start cutting, following the outline already marked. Try to be as exact as possible with your scissors.

10 The Sewing Machine

When the desired shapes have been cut out, stitch them together with the sewing machine following the manufacturer's directions.

11 Affixing Extras

Finally, sew on the hooks, buttons, and accessories by hand. At last, it's done!

The Finished Product!

Your costume, the only one of its kind in the world, is now ready to make its debut.

Cosplay Girls

Do It Yourself: Cosplay Salon

A lot of animation hairstyles are easier to draw than to wear. It might look impossible, but getting the hair right is the key to truly looking the part. It can only be done if you're willing to put in the time and effort.

Model: [*Yu-Gi-Oh!*] Yugi Muto

To Begin: Wash your hair with soap. Do not use any hair conditioner. What are a few split ends to a committed cosplayer? Ideally, the hair should be a little stiff but pliable.

1
With a fine-toothed comb, take strands of hair from the top of the head and tease them so that they stick up.

2
Holding each strand in place, spray from hair root to tip with hairspray.

3
When the top's done, do the same with the sides. The trick here is to twist the hair as you go.

4
Stick to the order of top, sides, then bottom. The bottom part, which needs to be done with the most care, can be time-consuming.

5
Pull and poke strands of hair into position to balance out the overall style.

6
From 6 to 8 inches away, give the whole head a good going over with the hairspray.

7
Except for the bangs, the basics are now finished.

8
This next part requires a lot of care, patience, and more hairspray. It's best to have a dryer handy too.

9
Again, tease the hair until it sticks out the way you want it. Here, however, spray only the roots so that it doesn't get too sticky.

The Finished Product!

It will probably take a whole can of hairspray, but the three-dimensional look is a real attention grabber. Remember: Avoid heavy gels and stick to spray.

Do It Yourself: Striking a Pose

When your costume is complete and your hair is done, it's time to practice working it for the cameras. No modeling experience? Studying the character you're portraying can help you develop an image and an attitude that can be worked into a number of poses. This is a crucial cosplay skill, and the more poses you perfect, the better.

Model: [*Virtua Fighter*] Sarah Bryant

Basic style: With one foot forward, slightly turn your body to make yourself appear thinner. This is important since most female characters have waists like underfed wasps.

Bend one leg and stretch the other out. The important thing here is to look away - you're mysterious and aloof.

For added sex appeal, turn your side to the camera and look back over your shoulder, chin up.

Looking Back: The key point here is the provocative look.

Fighting stance: Try to capture the energy and drama of the character here.

Kick pose: Practice by holding the position for 5 seconds at a time. It's harder than it looks, especially in platforms.

Work every nerve in your body, right down to the tips of your fingers. And however cool your character is, you're going to want to have some shots smiling.

Stand, crouch, sit...whatever you feel like, but make it look tough.

Use your hands, and with your head slightly cocked, try out different styles that suit you and your character.

Practice, Practice

Work on your moves in front of a full-length mirror. To make it look good you've got to become a little bit of a narcissist.

Cosplay Girls

Do It Yourself: Event Survival Tips

Attending an event is a must for any cosplayer worthy of her title. Events offer the chance for cosplayer and camera buffs, or cameko, to hang out together, have fun, pose, and shoot rolls of film. To get the most out of any event, be it at a park, convention hall, or club, follow these simple rules of conduct.

1 Get Into Character
Having changed into your costume and entered the event area, you are now in the world of cosplay. Shake off any shyness. You're here to have fun!

2 Photo Request
You may be stopped by cameko wanting to take your picture. Whether you accept or refuse is up to you.

3 Starting a Shoot
It's not unusual for cameko to want to take a number of shots. You can begin by simply standing, facing the camera.

4 Different Poses
Now you're ready to break out all those moves you've been practicing! Think about how you can express your character through the poses.

5 Checking the Snapshots
If the cameko's using a digital camera, let him know that you'd like to see the images as he takes them.

6 Name Card
If you're getting along, it's a good idea to exchange cards. In Japan, even the unemployed carry name cards. The cameko might send you some prints afterwards.

7 Ending a Shoot
When it's all over you might remain friends or choose never to see each other again. That's just how it goes at events.

What To Do When...

▲ The Cameko Starts Taking Photos Your Not Comfortable With

Tell him flat out "no!" "I'd like you to stop!" or "Sorry, but I'm not interested in those types of shots!" If he doesn't back off, ask someone around you to step in. Cosplayers always stick together at events.

Cameko Start Lining Up to Take Your Photo ▼

If you feel this is restricting you from moving around and enjoying the event, either refuse outright, or ask somebody nearby to count out loud to ten. Known as "The Count," this method is often used to warn over-eager cameko that their time is almost up.

Essentials

Money: To register and attend an event usually costs around 1,500 yen (around $12/50). And don't forget money for transportation and food.

Masking Tape/Safety Pins: Imperative for quick costume fixes. Super glue is also handy to have when a wing or a sword needs repair.

Name Card: When making new friends, it's convenient to have your cosplay photo, cos name, and e-mail address all on one card.

Mirror: Many of the changing-rooms are poorly equipped. Bring a small mirror just in case.

Camera: Bring your own if you want pictures. Most events don't sell cameras, and you may want to poach some costume ideas!

Candy/Snacks: Finding something to eat at an event can sometimes be difficult. Easy-to-carry energy boosters will get you through the day.

Cellular Phone: Important when planning to meet friends, or when trying to find the event itself.

Cosplay Girls

| Cosplayer Questionnaire | 1. What is Cosplay to You? | 2. What Do You Think of Cameko at Events? | 3. What Do You Dislike About Cosplay? |
| Cameko Questionnaire | 1. Why Do You Photograph Cosplayers? | 2. What Do You Think of Cosplayers? | 3. What's Your Cardinal Rule as a Cameko? |

Cosplayers

Cosplay isn't just about dressing up in costumes. For enthusiasts, it's seen as a form of self-expression as well as a way to socialize. In Japan, most cosplayers fall into the 15 to 30 age bracket, with females outnumbering males two to one. It takes a considerable amount of cash to cover the costs of attending events and making costumes, but as prices continue to drop, children as young as 10 are joining in.

A. Cos Name: "Kaede" (21)
Cosplay Career: 3 years, 10 months
1. It's a hobby.
2. I'd rather the cameko weren't there.
3. It's not really something I can go into...

B. Cos Name: "Hisho" (18)
Cosplay Career: 5 years, 4 months
1. It's my life.
2. I love them! They take great pictures of me.
3. Costumes cost a lot to make. I don't know what to do with my life.

C. Cos Name: "Kikunosuke" (18)
Cosplay Career: 5 months
1. It's helping me discover a lot about myself. The first event I ever attended was a cosplay contest. I won third prize, which was really cool.
2. They get in the way when they start lining up. And I don't like them taking sneak shots.
3. Cameko who give me the creeps but won't stop following me around.

D. Cos Name: "Yayoi" (24)
Cosplay Career: 4 years
1. It's stress relief.
2. I wish the cameramen didn't come.
3. I have to carry a lot of things, and then stand in line for a long time (at events).

E. Cos Name: "Kamyu" (19)
Cosplay Career: 4 years
1. I couldn't live without it.
2. They manage to make me look good.
3. Nothing...

F. Cos Name: "Noan" (21)
Cosplay Career: 3 years, 10 months
1. It's my hobby.
2. I don't like them being there.
3. I don't want anyone to know about what I do. Once I had my photo taken at an event, and I found out later that it appeared on the cover of some nerdy magazine that had nothing to do with cosplay.

G. Cos Name: "Marin" (16)
Cosplay Career: 3 months
1. I get to meet a lot of people.
2. No comment.
3. So far, nothing.

H. Cos Name: "Aki-ichi" (19)
Cosplay Career: 5 years
1. I couldn't survive without cosplay.
2. Most cameko seem to be there because they enjoy photography. I hate the ones who come just for the girls.
3. I spend so much money on cosplay that I'm always broke.

I. Cos Name: "Kanan" (23)
Cosplay Career: 6 years, 10 months
1. It's a fun thing to do. At an event once, I met a classmate who had no idea I was even into cosplay. We're now good friends.
2. I don't like the ones who are rude.
3. Sneak pictures!

 A
 B
 C
 D
 E
 F
 G
 H
 I

Cosplay Girls

Both Sides of the Camera

Cameko (Camera Kids)

Cameko, the amateur photographers at cosplay events, are mostly men in their twenties and thirties who have a special affection for the characters the cosplayers portray. As well as offering an opportunity to socialize, photography is another form of self-expression. Most turn up to events in their everyday clothes. In fact, a camera is all that's really needed; there's no special cameko certificate. Although they generally behave themselves, there are invariably those who see it as a chance to snap a few "dirty" pictures.

A. Cameko Name: "Yochiyochi G3" (45)
Cameko Career: 8 years
1. Their impulse to transform themselves is so human, and I want to capture it.
2. Cosplayers personify the multiple personalities that all humans have.
3. To take the best pictures I can.

B. Cameko Name: "Takanori Saito" (26)
Cameko Career: 1 year, 6 months
1. I like photography and I like anime. Also, there's something interesting about shooting somebody you know who's all made up.
2. There's something free about them. And through them I can follow my own dream.
3. To put everything into taking good photos.

C. Cameko Name: "Akihiro Koike" (46)
Cameko Career: 10 years, 10 months
1. It's a hobby. And I get to make friends with cute, nerdy girls.
2. They're part of my life.
3. Never try to pick the girls up.

D. Cameko Name: "Night Baron" (Age?)
Cameko Career: 5 years
1. I'm really into the *Sailor Moon* anime cosplay.
2. They're geeky expressionists.
3. Stick to *Sailor Moon*. *Sailor Moon* is all I shoot.

E. Cameko Name: "Masato Nebashi" (27)
Cameko Career: 7 years, 10 months
1. I like photographing beauty.
2. They're living in a dream.
3. To accurately depict beauty on film. By the way, I don't tell my colleagues at work that I'm a cameko. I got found out at my last job.

F. Cameko Name: "Togawa" (28)
Cameko Career: 5 years
1. I'm fascinated by their many facial expressions.
2. I'm here for photography. Just to observe and shoot.
3. Nothing really.

G. Cameko Name: "Kazuyoshi Miyazawa" (26)
Cameko Career: 2 years, 1 month
1. I enjoy looking at the different costumes. And I get to meet up with my cosplayer friends.
2. They're good people. They're a lot of fun to be with.
3. To be polite.

H. Cameko Name: "Mitsuharu Komaki" (36)
Cameko Career: 15 years
1. It's fun. Although there's some pushing and shoving from other cameko.
2. They're my friends.
3. Have fun taking pictures.

I. Cameko Name: "Mitsuharu Komaki" (38)
Cameko Career: 23 years
1. There's something interesting about fictitious characters coming to life.
2. Same as above.
3. As much as possible, to try to recreate on film the images of the characters.

Cosplay Girls

Cosplay Lingo

A

aikata (a-i-kata) *noun*
Cosplay partner who follows the same genre or title. Recently also used to talk about one's boyfriend/girlfriend.

Akiba (aki-ba) *noun*
Abbreviation for Akihabara, world famous electronics center crowded with stores of all sizes. Also known for it's many cosplay specialty shops.

all genre (all jan-ru) *noun.* Event with no limits regarding character, medium (manga, anime, game, etc), or activities. Mostly large-scale events where all cosplayers are welcome.

awase (awa-se) *noun*
Before cosplay event, the separation into groups of characters that appear together in different games, comics, etc.

C

cameko (came-ko) *noun*
Abbreviation of "Camera Kozo" (Camera Kid). An amateur photographer who shoots cosplayers at events.

CLAMP (clamp) *proper noun*
Chobits, Magic Knight Rayearth, Card Capter Sakura, etc.
Name of a manga club. Members, mostly women, produce manga, some of which have become extremely popular with cosplayers.

Comic Market (comic market) *proper noun*
Also known as "Comike," it's the largest amateur manga sales event in the world. Started in 1975, it is staged at Tokyo Big Sight each year in summer and winter. The events are known respectively as "Summer Comi" and "Winter Comi."

Comic Revolution (comic revolution) *proper noun*
Amateur manga event held at Ikebukuro's Sunshine Building and Tokyo Big Sight in spring and autumn. Usually called "C-Revo" or "Revo."

cos name (cos-name) *noun*
Nickname one uses at events or on-line. Cos names usually refer to a favorite character. Names can also be created by arranging different written kanji (ideograms) or sounds.

cosuru (cosu-ru) *verb*
To do cosplay.

cosplay shop (cosplay shop) *noun*
Shop selling cosplay goods such as costumes, accessories, etc. Some shops will take orders for costumes, while others will buy homemade costumes from their customers.

count (count) *noun*
A countdown used when too many cameko are crowding a popular cosplayer. Event staff or another cosplayer will usually say "Please make room after 5 seconds."

D

danpa (dan-pa) *noun*
Abbreviation for a cosplay dance party. Also known as "Cospa." Usually held at a rented disco or club.

dojin (dou-jin) *noun*
Person belonging to a manga circle which produces and publishes it's own amateur manga or novels.

dojinshi (dou-jin-shi) *noun*
Manga or novel produced by dojin.

E

event (iben-to) *noun*
Usually means "cosplay party event" for cosplayers. Held every sundays in Tokyo, once a month or two in other places.

I

ishoh (i-shou) *noun*
A costume, bought or hand made.

itai (i-tai) *adj*
Describes a person lacking courtesy and manner to others. Used for cosplayers and cameko.

K

karakoro (kara-koro) *noun*
A small hand-pulled cart used to carry cosplay gear such as costumes, props, etc.

korobu (koro-bu) *verb*
To fall over. Implies liking a character, game, genre, etc, so much as to "fall" for it.

L

layer (lay-ah) *noun*
Someone who does cosplay. Abbreviation of "cosplayer."

M

manga (man-ga) *noun*
Japanese comic books and novels.

moe (mo-e) *adjective*
Opposite of "nae." Describes a character with which one is infatuated. Also used to express passion.

N

nae (na-e) *adjective*
Opposite of "moe." Describes a character with which one has fallen out of love.

nagamono (naga-mono) *noun*
Commonly used name for cosplay accessories such as swords or canes. Although an important character trade-mark, they are banned at some events.

O

only event (only event) *noun*
Dojin event specializing in a certain medium, such as anime, manga, or games, or a particular character or pairing of characters.

otaku (ota-ku) *noun*
Someone with an obsessive interest in anime, manga, etc. More than just a fan.

P

peep (peep) *verb*
A photo taken without the subject's permission. Such shots are usually uncomplimentary. Sometimes photos are even taken in the changing rooms.

S

satsueikai (satsu-ay-kai) *noun*
A get-together photo shooting party, using props and sets. Some are held by character fans, and some are held by cameko who just want to shoot cute girls with outfits.

shugo (shu-go) *noun*
A get-together. Refers to cosplayer followers of the same character getting together for a group photo. These photo ops are particularly popular on cosplaying couples' birthdays.

T

Tokyo Big Sight (tokyo big sight) *proper noun*
Japan's largest and most well known trade convention hall. Located in Tokyo. Nearest stations are Kokusai-tenjijo-mae on the Yurikamome Line and Kokusai-tenjijo on the Rinkai Line. At Comic Market events, the hall is packed with cosplayers.

torareta (tora-reta) *noun*
Describes a cosplayer who goes out of his/her way to attract the photographers' attention, either by their actions or their revealing costume.

W

wig (wig-u) *noun*
A cosplay essential for recreating the hairstyle and color of the character. There are countless styles, lengths, and colors to choose from.

Y

yaoi (ya-o-i) *noun*
A genre with a mostly female following that depicts homosexual male romances.

Essai's Scrapbook:
Cosplay Then and Now

ESSAI USHIJIMA
Essai Ushijima's fascination with cosplay began 30 years ago, when, as a three year-old, he made his debut dressed as super hero Kamen Rider. By the age of 12 he had fallen under the spell of the *Urusei Yatsura* anime character Ozuno Tsubame, and was hooked. Today, as well as managing cosplay events, he lectures and writes about his lifelong passion.

Cosplay, like any movement, has its fair share of fanzines, fan clubs and hero-worship. Popular culture - from kabuki and theater to film and music - has always attracted enthusiasts who like to dress as their idols do. Today's youth, and even many parents, have grown up on a TV diet of animation.

Costumed hordes at the annual Tokyo Comic Market Convention.

Therefore, choosing to idolize a cartoon character isn't so strange. A fan of rock music will don a leather jacket and grow his hair long. A more conservative woman might wear a suit. Broadly speaking, these are also forms of cosplay. For fans of anime, manga and computer games it's simply an affirmation of their tastes.

Uniforms

Military-wear runs the gamut from ancient to modern and authentic to S+M.

A Cosplay Revolution

Although it didn't have a name at the time, cosplay probably dates back to the 1930s, when train enthusiasts took to dressing up as railway workers. In the mid-sixties, Japan's first Sci-Fi conventions from overseas led to homegrown events a few years later that featured alien masquerades. But it wasn't until 1975 that a group of aficionados costumed themselves as their favorite characters to promote their manga circle, and cosplay made the crossover into the world of comics. Soon after, the first real cosplayers emerged, inspired by Glam fashion, boys-wear and army surplus. Since then, uniforms have become a cosplay genre, with faux-waitresses and adult schoolchildren joining the ranks of station guards and soldiers. The Gothic-Lolita boom is the most recent of influences. Over the past two years cosplaying girls have increasingly been taking to the streets dressed as frilly maids.

Essai's Scrapbook: Cosplay Then and Now
Animation & Comics

as Sakura Kinomoto and Kero from *Card Captor Sakura* circa 2000

as Runa Kouzuki and Casshan from *Casshan: Robot Hunter* circa 1998

from *Porco Rosso* circa 1999

as Bloodberry, Lime, Otaru Mamiya and Cherry from *Saber Marionette* circa 1998

from *Doraemon* circa 1999

from *The Oh My Goddess* circa 1998

from *Future GPX Cyber Formula* circa 1997

as Araune from *Witch Girl Vivian* circa 1999

as Maetel from *Galaxy Express 999* circa 1998

from *Rurouni Kenshin* circa 1997

Homemade Costumes:
Inspired by Anime and Manga

The first anime cosplay to appear on the scene was *Umi no Toriton* at the 1977 Comic Market. The release of *Uchu Senkan Yamato* soon after led to the first cosplay boom. But it wasn't until *Kido Senshi Gundam* came along that the anime cosplay boom really took off. At events held at the time, half the guests would turn up in the same anime costume. Gundam's popularity lasted through to the early '90s, eclipsed only when *Saint Seiya* became a hit. This fascination with the very unreal world of anime and manga required clothing that simply didn't exist. Homemade costumes and accessories were the answer.

As anime and manga productions increase, more and more characters are entering into the cosplay world. Recent works that never fail to catch on include characters established with cosplay in mind. The reissuing of decades-old comics has further widened the field. The newest of this cosplay genre pays homage to the anime characters of the late '70s, such as *Yattaman*.

as Mai Shiranui from *Garo Densetsu* circa 1998

as Athena Asamiya from *King of Fighters* circa 1998

as Mai Shiranui from *Garo Densetsu* circa 1999

as Bad man from *Virtua Cop* circa 1999

as Honey from *Fighting Vipers* circa 1998

as Nakoruru from *Samurai Shadow* circa 1997

as Mai Shiranui from *Garo Densetsu* circa 1999

as Yuka Takeuchi from *VariableGeo* circa 1998

as Lisa Kusanami from *Last Bronx* circa 1999

Being the Star: The Popularity of GameCosplay

When the street-fighter game boom hit Japan at the start of the '90s the parallel cosplay genre exploded. Unlike anime and manga, video games allowed the cosplayers to "become" their characters, making it all the more real. Each fighter even had his or her own personal history. Girls in particular were wowed by the hard-nosed female characters, such as Chun-Li from *Street Fighter 2* and Nakoruru from *Samurai Shodown*. The simplicity of the costumes is also a big attraction. In many cases everyday clothes can be worked into the overall design, saving time and money.

as Queen Angelique and Clavis from *Angelique2* circa 2000

as Sakura Shinguji from *Sakura Wars* circa 1999

as Sakura Shinguji from *Sakura Wars* circa 1999

from *Tokimeki Memorial* circa 1999

as Sakura Shinguji, Sumire Kanzaki, Iris Chateaubriand and Ri Kohran from *Sakura Wars* circa 1999

as Oscar from *Angelique* circa 2000

as Hero and Sage female from *Dragon Warrior* circa 1997

from *Sakura Wars* circa 1999

RPG:
So Many Characters to Choose From

RPGs (Role Playing Games) appeared in the mid-90s just as interest in manga and anime was fading. They soon became all the rage, as reflected by their cosplay popularity. With games such as *Dragon Warrior* and *Final Fantasy* leading the genre, RPGs continue to be popular today. Although they allow a more "real" relationship with the character than anime and manga, much of their success in cosplay is due to the many characters available to choose from. More recently, characters from RPGs that combine war simulation, such as *Sakura Wars* and *Gun Parade March*, are attracting a following.

YATTAMAN NI-GO

Special thanks to SMILE-KAN   1-44 Kanda Jimbocho, Chiyoda-ku, Tokyo   Tel:03-5283-3377

This costume is old-school Japanese animation from the 1970's. Lots of cosplayers are drawing on the classics these days for their fun designs as well as their sentimental value.

Also available from cocoro books

Japanese Movie Posters

Monster and Yakuza, Ghosts and Samurai, Anime, Pink and New Cinema!

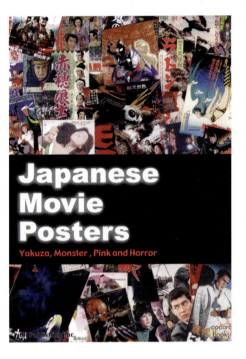

A tribute to 50 years of lurid imagery and purple prose created by nameless designers at Japanese film studios. Unforgettable images conjured out of a few still photos, some bold lettering, and plenty of tattoos, swords, guns, baseball bats, ropes, scowls, leers, scars, rubber suits, school uniforms, cartoon characters, and half-naked women.
ISBN 0-9723124-0-4

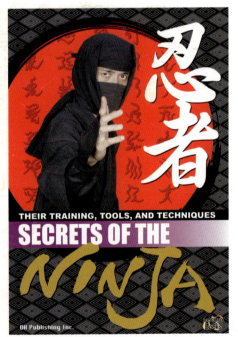

SECRETS OF THE NINJA

THEIR TRAINING, TOOLS, AND TECHNIQUES

Now you see them, now you don't. Peek inside the ninja's world and discover the skills, weapons, and ingenious tricks that made these men and women feared and revered for centuries. You'll learn their ancient codes as well as techniqus for meditation, stealth, and generally fighting dirty.
ISBN 0-9723124-1-2

Check out more great books from cocoro books and DH Publishing on our website

http://www.dhp-online.com

e-mail customer@dhp-online.com to receive our e-mail newsletter.